146

114

172

Freigegeben durch OLF.

Luftwaffe
Propaganda Postcards

**A PICTORIAL HISTORY
IN ORIGINAL GERMAN POSTCARDS**

JAMES WILSON

Airlife
England

This book is dedicated to the memory of my father,
an honourable man, and my inspiration.

First published in the UK in 1996
by Airlife Publishing Ltd

British Library Cataloguing in Publication Data
  A catalogue record for this book
  is available from the British Library

ISBN 1 85310 727 1

Design: J V A Wilson
Artwork and typesetting: J Gilbert

Printed in England by Livesey Ltd, Shrewsbury

Airlife Publishing Ltd
101 Longden Road, Shrewsbury SY3 9EB, England

Luftwaffe Propaganda Postcards

The Luftwaffe came into being on 30 January 1933, when Adolf Hitler, the new Chancellor of Germany, appointed Hermann Göring Minister of Aviation that same day. The Luftwaffe would remain a secret force for a further two years until March 1935, when Hitler officially announced its existence in defiance of the Treaty of Versailles, which denied Germany the right to an air force.

Having developed tactics and strategy which they were able to put into practice with the Condor Legion during the Spanish Civil War (between July 1936 and March 1939), the Luftwaffe had gained a distinct advantage through this experience when the Second World War began in September 1939. As for the French, tactics were virtually non-existent as far as air warfare was concerned and the British for their part were still using those learnt during the First World War.

As a result, the Luftwaffe was probably the most modern and powerful air force of its time, and Third Reich propaganda efficiency inspired the nation by producing photographic postcards on a scale unthought of by any other military power.

The dramatic settings, together with the overall superb quality of these postcards, provides us with not only an interesting piece of history, but also some stunning images of the men and machines of Hitler's Luftwaffe which dominated the skies of Europe during the early years of the Second World War.

Taking into account the passage of time since these postcards were produced, it is indeed surprising that so many survive, bearing in mind that their content and appeal would not have been so great after the war, many having been destroyed in one way or another.

Finally, it should be noted that the area of perhaps greatest importance, Germany's development of rocket and jet powered aircraft later in the war, was not widely covered by postcards, if at all. To date, nothing has surfaced in this particular area, but, the search continues!

Contents

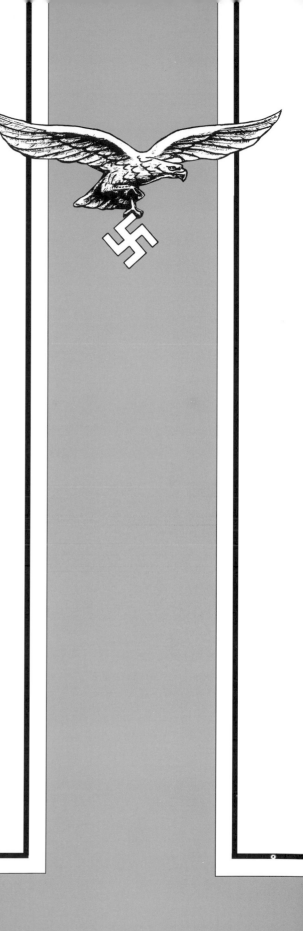

Wasserkuppe

This monument bears an inscription which honours the memory of fallen German airmen of the 1914-18 War. It is situated at Wasserkuppe in the Rhön area of central Germany, which was the home of gliding schools long before Adolf Hitler became Chancellor.

WIR
TOTEN FLIEGER BLIEBEN
SIEGER
DVRCH VNS ALLEIN
VOLK
FLIEG DV WIEDER
VND DV WIRST
SIEGER
DVRCH DICH
ALLEIN

1

2

The gliders passing over the monument bear the national symbol following 1933. It was here that many future pilots of the Luftwaffe were introduced to flying.

Arado – Ar 66

Manufactured by Arado Flugzeugwerke GmbH in 1932, the Ar 66 was one of the main training aircraft of a still secret Luftwaffe. It entered service with the training schools in 1933, and continued in this role well into the war. About 10,000 were built in different versions. The aircraft remained in use until 1945 for night-attack and harassment duties.

   With a crew of two, pilot and pupil, the Ar 66 had a maximum speed of 130 mph and a ceiling of just under 15,000 ft. Originally the aircraft had no armament, but later versions allowed the carriage of light bombs.

3

4

Sportflugzeug Arado Ar. 66 C

5

Arado – Ar 68

Manufactured in 1933 as a single-seat fighter, the Ar 68 entered service in 1936 and was the last biplane fighter to enter Luftwaffe service. It did see some limited use as a night fighter during the war, but by this time most were in use at advanced training schools.

The Ar 68 had a maximum speed of just over 200 mph and a ceiling of 26,500 ft. Armament consisted of two MG17 machine-guns firing forward, together with up to six 22 lb fragmentation bombs.

Arado Ar 68

6

Durchdrehen des Motors

7

Motor wird auf Kompression gedreht

8

Die Bremsklötze werden fortgezogen

9

Eine stolze Staffel

10

Arado – Ar 79

Manufactured in 1938 as a two-seat (side by side) light training aircraft, the Ar 79 had a maximum speed of just over 140 mph and a service ceiling of some 18,000 ft.
It was unarmed.

D-EKCX

Schul- und Reiseflugzeug ARADO Ar 79

11

Arado Ar 79

Arado – Ar 95

Designed as a torpedo bomber and reconnaissance aircraft, this floatplane first appeared in 1936, and saw some use on the Eastern Front during the war. A version with a wheeled undercarriage, the Ar 95B, reached prototype stage but never went into production owing to its poor performance.

With a crew of two, pilot and observer/gunner, the Ar 95 had a maximum speed of 190 mph and a service ceiling of around 24,000 ft. Armament consisted of a single MG17 machine-gun firing forward, and one MG15 machine-gun on a movable mounting in the rear of the cockpit, together with one torpedo or one bomb of over 800 lb and six smaller bombs of 100 lb on wing racks.

14

Arado Ar 95

15

16

Arado – Ar 96B

Produced in 1938 as an advanced trainer, this was one of the most important training aircraft in use with the Luftwaffe from 1940 onwards. Certain modified versions of the Ar 96B carried bombs to train pilots in dive-bombing and ground-attack. Production continued in some countries after 1945, and over 11,000 were built during the war.

With a pilot and pupil the Ar 96B had a maximum speed of just over 200 mph and a ceiling of around 23,000 ft. Armament consisted of one MG17 machine-gun firing forward, although some were fitted with a second MG17 in the rear cockpit for training air gunners.

Arado Ar 96 B

17

Übungsflugzeug Arado Ar 96 B.

18

Arado – Ar 196

Originating in 1938, the Ar 196 first entered service in late 1939. It was designed to operate from naval vessels, but it was also used successfully by coastal patrol stations for reconnaissance and anti-shipping duties.

Crewed by a pilot and observer/gunner, the Ar 196 had a maximum speed of over 190 mph and a service ceiling of just under 23,000 ft. Armament consisted of two 20 mm cannon and two MG17 machine-guns, one firing forward and the other on a movable mounting firing to the rear, plus two bombs of over 100 lb each. Approximately 500 of these aircraft were built.

19

Bordkunder Arado Ar 196 auf dem Katapult

20

PK-Aufnahme: Aubele (Sch)

21

Blohm & Voss – BV 138

First produced by Blohm & Voss Abt Flugzeugbau in 1937 as a flying boat for long-range maritime reconnaissance, the BV 138 also served as transport, and some were converted for a minesweeping role. Proving itself a very seaworthy craft, it operated in most areas during the war, and about 280 were produced.

With a crew of two pilots, an observer, an engineer and a radio operator (gunner), the BV 138 had a maximum speed of 145 mph and a service ceiling of almost 32,000 ft.

Armament on the final C1 version consisted of two 20 mm cannon in turrets, one in the hull and another in the bows, plus one MG131 machine-gun behind the central engine and a further MG15 in a starboard position. The bomb load varied from a maximum of six 110 lb bombs on wing racks to four 331 lb depth charges.

22

Bücker – Bü 131 "Jungmann"

Produced by Bücker Flugzeugbau GmbH in 1934 as a trainer, the Bü 131 entered service with Luftwaffe training schools in 1935 and continued in use until the end of the war. When they were replaced to some extent by the Bü 181 after 1939 some Bü 131s found their way to the Eastern Front, where they were used in the ground/night-attack roles.

With a pilot and pupil the Bü 131 had a maximum speed of over 110 mph and a ceiling of almost 10,000 ft. In the training role it was unarmed.

Militär-Schulflugzeug Bü 131 „Jungmann"

23

Bücker – Bü 133 "Jungmeister"

First produced in 1935 as an advanced training aircraft, the Bü 133 incorporated many features of the Bü 131 and its wonderful aerobatic qualities made it an excellent aircraft for training fighter pilots.

With a pilot and pupil the Bü 133 had a maximum speed of almost 140 mph and a ceiling of just over 14,750 ft. It was unarmed.

Übungseinsitzer Bü 133 „Jungmeister"

24

Übungseinsitzer Bücker „Jungmeister" Bü 133 C mit Bramo Sh 14 A Motor

25

Bücker – Bü 180 "Student"

Originating in 1938, the Bü 180 was a dual-control primary trainer with aerobatic capabilities. Although it was intended for civil use only, it is possible that some would-be Luftwaffe pilots received initial training in this aircraft, which lent its basic design characteristics to later military training aircraft, namely the Bü 181 "Bestmann".

With a crew of pilot and pupil the Bü 180 had a maximum speed of almost 110 mph, a ceiling of 14,760 ft and a range of just over 400 miles. It was unarmed, and production was limited to small numbers.

BÜCKER-Student

26

Dornier – Do 11

Manufactured by Dornier-Werke GmbH, the Do 11 of 1932 was designed as a heavy bomber, but at the time was termed a 'freight carrier' as it was being built contrary to the Treaty of Versailles. The Do 11 was used in long-distance navigation experiments by the then-secret Luftwaffe and played an important role in those early years, but it was outdated by the outbreak of war in 1939.

Crewed by a pilot, observer, engineer/gunner and radio operator/gunner, the Do 11 had a maximum speed of 160 mph and a ceiling of around 13,500 ft.
Armament consisted of three MG15 machine-guns, one forward, one in a dorsal position and one in the belly of the aircraft, plus a bomb load of some 2,200 lb.

Echt Foto

27

Dornier-Zweimotoren-Kampfflugzeug

28

29

30

31

32

Dornier – Do 17

Originating in 1934 and known as the 'flying pencil' because of its slender fuselage, the Do 17 was originally designed as a civil transport/mailplane and was delivered to the Luftwaffe as a medium-range bomber in 1936. The aircraft was used successfully during the Spanish Civil War by the Condor Legion, and saw service in France, Poland, the Balkans and Britain during the early years of the war, After 1943, however, it was used mainly for second-line, training and reconnaissance duties.

With a crew of three, comprising pilot, observer and radio operator/gunner, the Do 17 had a maximum speed of 220 mph and a ceiling of just under 17,000 ft.

Its armament consisted of two MG15 machine-guns, one firing forward and down, and the other firing aft together with a bomb load of 1,700 lb.

The Do 17M & Z models, manufactured in 1939, had six MG15 machine-guns and a crew of four including an engineer/ gunner. This aircraft had a maximum speed of 190 mph and a ceiling of just under 27,000 ft.

33

34

35

36

37

Kampfflugzeug Dornier Do 17
Blick aus dem Schützenstand

38

39

Dornier – Do 18

Designed as a long-range mailplane to replace the Do15 "Wal", the Do 18 first appeared in 1935 and was used in a number of roles including reconnaissance, patrol, air-sea rescue and anti-shipping.

With a crew of pilot, observer, engineer/gunner and radio operator/gunner, it had a maximum speed of over 160 mph and a service ceiling of just under 14,000 ft. Armament consisted of one forward MG131 machine-gun and one MG151 machine-gun in a dorsal position, plus the capacity to carry two bombs of over 100 lb each beneath the wings. About 150 of these aircraft were built.

40

Dornier Langstreckenflugboot Do 18 D ANHR führte im Dienste der Deutschen Lufthansa 1936 die ersten planmäßigen Verkehrsflüge über den Nordatlantik durch, steht seitdem auch im regelmäßigen Dienst nach Südamerika. Vom 27.—29. 3. 38 wurde durch die Besatzung Flugkapitän von Engel, Flugzeugführer Gundermann, Funkmaschinist Rösel und Flugzeugfunker Stein mit dem Flugboot Do 18 D ANHR der internationale Langstreckenrekord für Wasserflugzeuge auf der Strecke Start Point (engl. Kanalküste) — Caravellas (Brasilien) mit einer Strecke von 8500 km für Deutschland erobert. Abmessungen: Spannweite 23,7 m, Länge 19,25 m, Flügelfläche 98 qm.

41

42

Dornier – Do 24

The Do 24 flying boat which first appeared in 1937, was used for air-sea rescue and transport duties, seeing service during the invasion of Norway and being used in most coastal areas.

Approximately 300 were built during the war in all versions, and the Do 24 continued to be produced outside Germany under licence until the 1960s.

With a six-man crew comprising two pilots, an observer, an engineer, a radio operator/gunner and a gunner, it had a maximum speed of over 200 mph and a ceiling of 24,600 ft.

Its armament consisted of two MG15 machine-guns in front and rear turrets, together with a 20 mm cannon in a dorsal position.

Seenotflugboot Dornier Do 24

43

Dornier – Do 26

The Do 26 of 1938 was a flying boat designed for transport and long-range reconnaissance. Although production was limited to a very small number, it did see service with the Luftwaffe, mainly in Norway.

Crewed by a pilot, observer, radio operator/gunner and engineer/gunner, the Do 26 had a maximum speed of over 180 mph and an altitude limit of almost 15,000 ft. Its armament consisted of three MG15 machine-guns, two in turrets either side of the fuselage and a third in the rear, together with a 20 mm cannon in a front turret.

Seefernaufklärer-Flugboot Dornier Do 26

44

Dornier – Do 215

The Do 215 was the designation given to the export version of the Do 17Z produced in 1939. The Do 215 had a four-man crew comprising pilot, observer, radio operator/gunner and engineer/gunner. It had a maximum speed of 240 mph and a ceiling of 29,500ft.

The armament and bomb load remained the same as that of the Do 17Z, but a later version, the Do 215B, had two 20mm cannon and four MG17 machine-guns. This aircraft saw limited service in the night-fighter, intruder and reconnaissance roles.

Kampfflugzeug Dornier Do 215

45

Do 215

46

47

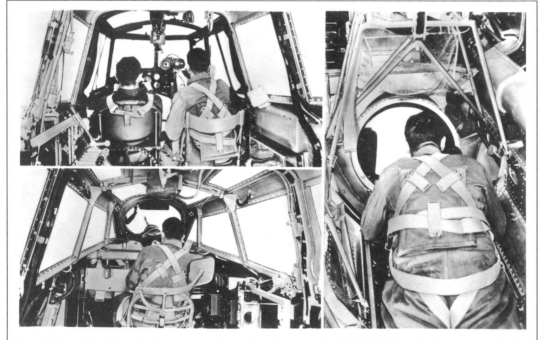

48

Fieseler – Fi 156 "Storch"

First produced in 1936 by Gerhard Fieseler Werke GmbH, the Fi 156 was used in a variety of roles: communications, observation, liaison, rescue and air ambulance. This extremely versatile aircraft operated successfully in all of these roles and on all fronts, having the ability to land and take off on short, makeshift landing strips. Entering service with the Luftwaffe in 1937, it continued in use until the end of the war when some 2,500 had been built. It is best known for its use in the daring rescue of Mussolini from Gran Sasso by the Germans in September 1943, following his dismissal and imprisonment by the new Italian government in July that year. With a crew of up to three the Fi 156 had a maximum speed of 110 mph and a ceiling of over 15,000 ft. Armament consisted of one MG15 machine-gun on adjustable mounting in rear of cockpit.

49

Fi 156 „Storch"

50

Fi 156 „Storch"

Fieseler – Fi 167

The Fi 167, which first appeared in 1938, was originally designed for aircraft carrier use, but following the shelving of Germany's carrier programme they were used for coastal exercises. Most of the small number completed were sold to the Romanians.

With a crew of two, pilot and observer/gunner, the Fi 167 had a maximum speed of almost 200 mph and a service ceiling of almost 25,000 ft.

Its armament consisted of two MG17 machine-guns, one firing forward and the other on an adjustable mounting firing aft together with a bomb load of 2,200 lb or one torpedo of around 1,700 lb.

Fieseler Mehrzweckflugzeug

51

52

Focke-Wulf – Fw 44 "Stieglitz"

First produced by Focke-Wulf Flugzeugbau GmbH in 1932, the Fw 44 was used at Luftwaffe training schools everywhere throughout the war. Carrying a pilot and pupil, the Fw 44 had a maximum speed of 115 mph and an altitude limit of almost 13,000 ft. It was unarmed.

Schul-, Sport- und Kunstflugzeug Focke-Wulf Fw 44 "Stieglitz"

53

1 Staffel Fw. 44 "Stieglitz"

54

Echte Fotografie

F. W. Stieglitz

55

Unsere Luftwaffe
Vor dem Start

56

Focke-Wulf Fw 44 „Stieglitz"

57

Courtesy: Lawrence collection.

Focke-Wulf Fw. 44 „Stieglitz"

58

Focke-Wulf – Fw 56 "Stösser"

The Fw 56 of 1933 was designed as a defensive fighter, but was used as an advanced trainer for fighter pilots following its relegation from front-line duties before the outbreak of war. Approximately 1,000 were built.

A single-seater, the Fw 56 had a maximum speed of almost 170 mph and a ceiling of over 20,000 ft. Armament consisted of two MG17 machine-guns and it could carry three bombs of over 20 lb each.

Focke-Wulf   Fw 56 „Stößer"

59

Focke-Wulf Fw. 56 „Stösser"

60

Focke-Wulf FW 56 „Stoesser"

61

Courtesy: Lawrence collection.

Focke-Wulf – Fw 58 "Weihe"

First produced in 1935 as a transport and training aircraft, the versatile Fw 58 also saw use as a communications and air-ambulance aircraft. It could carry up to six passengers, but its range was somewhat limited, being about 500 miles. Approximately 4,500 were delivered to the Luftwaffe, some of which were fitted with floats.

With a crew of up to four, consisting of pilot, observer and two gunners, the Fw 58 had a maximum speed of over 160 mph and a service ceiling of over 18,000 ft.

The armament varied, ranging from none at all to two machine-guns, one firing forward and a second on movable mounting rear of the cockpit, plus a small bomb load.

62

Focke-Wulf Fw 58 „Weihe"

63

Kampfbrunit

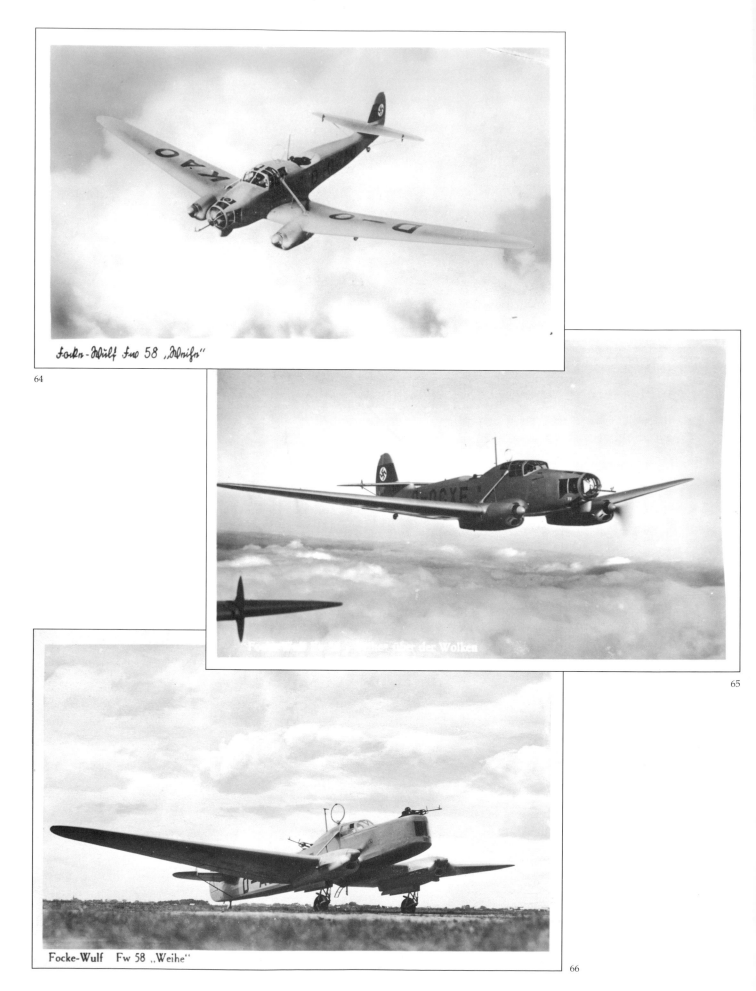

Focke-Wulf Fw 58 „Weihe"

64

Focke-Wulf Fw 58 „Weihe" über der Wolken

65

Focke-Wulf   Fw 58 „Weihe"

66

Focke-Wulf Fw 58 „Weihe"

67

Focke-Wulf Fw 58 „Weihe"

68

Focke-Wulf
Fw 58
,,Weihe''

69

Focke-Wulf – Fw 187 "Falke"

Designed as a heavy fighter, the Fw 187 first appeared in 1937 and was indeed very fast and manoeuvrable, and should have been assured of its place amongst the best Luftwaffe aircraft, however this was not to be, owing to a lack of interest by the Reichsluftfahrministerium (RLM), and despite very impressive trials, production did not proceed. The completed half-dozen or so aircraft were kept as a defence force at Focke-Wulf's Bremen plant.

With a crew of two, pilot and observer, the Fw 187 reached a maximum speed of 390 mph and had a ceiling of almost 33,000 ft. Its armament consisted of two 20 mm cannon and four MG17 machine-guns.

70

Focke-Wulf – Fw 189 "Uhu"

Produced in 1938 for reconnaissance and army co-operation use, the Fw 189 was very successful in these roles, particularly on the Eastern Front and in the Middle East. Some 860 were produced for the Luftwaffe.

With a crew of pilot, observer and gunner the Fw 189 had a maximum speed of over 200 mph and a service ceiling of almost 23,000 ft. Its armament consisted of two MG17 machine-guns firing forward and four MG81 machine-guns, two firing from dorsal positions and two in the rear, together with an external bomb load of four bombs of over 100 lb each.

Focke-Wulf Nahaufklärer Fw 189

71

Unsere Luftwaffe. Focke-Wulf Nahaufklärer Fw 189

72

Focke-Wulf Aufklärung "Fw 189"

73

Focke-Wulf – Fw 190

Originating in 1939, the Fw 190 was probably the most successful German fighter aircraft of the Second World War. Designed by Kurt Tank, it was intended to replace the Bf 109 which it did, but never completely. The Fw 190 first entered service with the Luftwaffe in early 1941. A very tough single-seater, it was capable of operating from rough front-line airstrips on the Eastern Front, among other areas. Some versions were fitted with bad weather/night flying equipment, radar and autopilot, and over 20,000 were built in all versions. Performance was steadily improved through these versions, until finally it had a maximum speed of almost 360 mph and a service ceiling of almost 39,500 ft.

Armament consisted of two MG17 machine-guns and two 20 mm cannon together with bomb loads of between 550 and 1,100 lb. Rockets were carried in some instances.

74

41

75

76

Focke-Wulf – Fw 200 "Condor"

The Fw 200, which first appeared in 1937, was originally designed as a long-range commercial transport aircraft, but it entered service with the Luftwaffe in the reconnaissance, anti-shipping and transport roles. It was used very successfully in the anti-shipping role during the early war years, particularly in the Atlantic where it was used as a flying homing-beacon to guide the U-boats to the convoys. However the aircraft suffered heavily following the introduction of escort carriers to protect the convoy routes. The Fw 200 was also used as a transport in the relief of Stalingrad, but it was never built in large numbers, approximately 275 being used by the Luftwaffe.

With a seven-man crew, comprising pilot, co-pilot, radio operator, observer, engineer and two gunners, one of whom also acted as radar operator, the Fw 200 had a maximum speed of 225 mph and a ceiling of almost 20,000 ft. Its armament consisted of two MG15 machine-guns, three MG131 machine-guns and a single 20 mm cannon, together with a bomb load of 4,600 lb.

77

Focke-Wülf Fernkampfflugzeug Fw 200 L „Condor".

78

Langstreckenbomber Fw 200 C. „Condor"

79

Fernkampfbomber Focke Wulf Fw. 200-C. „Condor"

80

Heinkel – He 45

Produced in 1932 by Ernst Heinkel A.G. as a reconnaissance bomber and training aircraft, the He 45 was outdated when war broke out, but it did see limited front-line service in the night-attack role. Some 500 were built for the Luftwaffe.

Carrying a pilot and observer/gunner the He 45 had a maximum speed of 180 mph and a ceiling of just over 18,000 ft. It was armed with two MG17 machine-guns, one firing forward and the other on a movable mounting in the rear cockpit.

Übung am Flugzeug

81

Heinkel – He 46

The He 46 first appeared in 1931 and entered service with the Luftwaffe in 1934. As a short-range reconnaissance and army co-operation aircraft it played an important part during the early build-up of the Luftwaffe. The He 46 saw service during the Spanish Civil War, and although it was largely replaced by the Henschel Hs 126 after 1938 it continued in use on the Eastern Front until 1943 in the night-attack and harassment roles. It was not produced in large numbers, some 480 being built.

With a crew of pilot and observer/gunner, the He 46 had a maximum speed of over 150 mph and a ceiling of almost 20,000 ft. Its armament consisted of one MG17 machine-gun on a movable mounting in the rear cockpit, plus a bomb load of almost 450 lb.

82

BEFEHLSAUSGABE VOR DEM AUFKLÄRUNGSFLUG

83

Heinkel – He 51

A single-seat fighter, the He 51 originated in 1933 and saw service in Spain with the Condor Legion, where it was used quite successfully. Over 700 were built in different versions, some being fitted with floats, but by 1938 the type had been relegated to fighter pilot training duties.

The He 51 had a maximum speed of just over 200 mph and a service ceiling of over 25,000 ft. Armament consisted of two MG17 machine-guns.

84

85

86

87

88

89

Heinkel – He 59

Designed as a torpedo bomber and reconnaissance floatplane (although some prototypes had a wheeled undercarriage), the He 59 first appeared in 1931 and was used successfully in a number of roles, namely coastal mining, rescue, ground-attack, reconnaissance, training and the insertion of agents. It saw operational service in the Spanish campaign and was still in use in 1943.

With a crew consisting of pilot, observer, radio operator/gunner and gunner the He 59 had a maximum speed of almost 140 mph and a ceiling of 11,500 ft. It carried three MG15 machine-guns, one in the nose, one in a dorsal position and a third in the belly of the aircraft, plus a bomb load of just over 2,200 lb or a single torpedo of equivalent weight.

90

Unsere Luftwaffe
Wasserflugzeug

91

Die hinteren Kampfstände eines Heinkel-Seeflugzeuges

92

Heinkel – He 60

First produced in 1933 as a short-range reconnaissance floatplane to operate from warships (which it did until replaced by the Arado Ar 196 towards the end of 1939), the He 60 remained in service until 1943 for reconnaissance duties from coastal stations. Approximately 250 were built.

With a two-man crew of pilot and observer/gunner, it had a maximum speed of 140 mph and a ceiling of almost 16,500 ft. Its armament consisted of a single MG15 machine-gun on a movable mounting in the rear cockpit.

Wasserflugzeug wird an Bord genommen   A. Klein

93

Flugzeug wird mit Hilfe eines Demag-Bordwippkranes an Bord genommen

94

Startende Kette von Wasserflugzeugen

A. Klein

95

96

Heinkel – He72 "Kadett"

Originating in 1933 and widely used in Luftwaffe training schools, the He 72 saw service in the communications and reconnaissance roles during the early part of the war.

With a pilot and pupil/observer the unarmed He 72 had a maximum speed of 115 mph and a ceiling of 11,500 ft.

Heinkel - Übungsflugzeug He 72 »Kadett«

97

Heinkel – He 111

The He 111 medium bomber, which first appeared in 1935, became the Luftwaffe's main bomber for most of the War. Having a range of around 750 miles, it was produced in large numbers, some 7,000 being built in all versions. The He 111 saw service during the Spanish Civil War and on all fronts throughout the War, not only as a bomber but also in the roles of anti-shipping (which included dropping torpedoes), transport, paratroop dropping and the air-launching of V1 rockets.

The final version, the He 111-H16, had a crew of five, comprising pilot, observer, radio operator/gunner, engineer/gunner and gunner. It had a maximum speed of approximately 250 mph and a ceiling of almost 29,000 ft. This version was armed with two 20 mm cannon or one MG15 machine-gun in the nose, one MG131 machine-gun in a dorsal position, two MG81 machine-guns in the belly to the rear, and two MG15 or MG81s in the fuselage sides, plus a bomb load of some 7,200 lb.

Kampfflugzeug wird mit Bomben beladen

98

99

Heinkel-Kampfflugzeug He 111

100

101

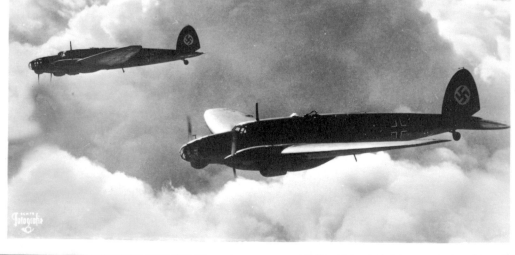

102

103

104

105

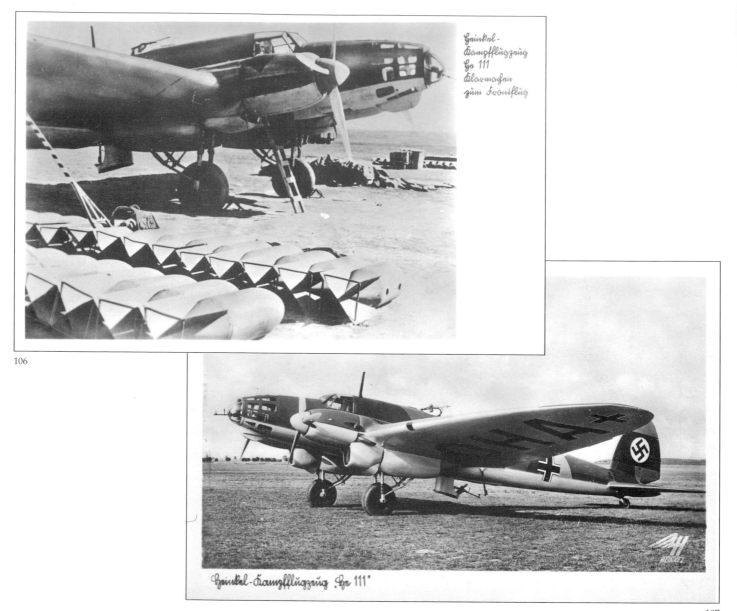

Heinkel-
Kampfflugzeug
He 111
Klarmachen
zum Frontflug

106

Heinkel-Kampfflugzeug "He 111"

107

108

Heinkel-
Kampfflugzeug
He 111
Bombenabwurf

109

110

111   Heinkel-Kampfflugzeug He 111

112

Das Gesicht des Heinkel-Kampfflugzeuges He 111   Freigegeben durch OLF.

113

114   So sieht der Flugzeugführer der Heinkel-He 111 seinen Kettenkamerad   Freigegeben durch OLF.

115   Eine Kette Heinkel-Kampfflugzeuge He 111   Freigegeben durch OLF.

Heinkel – He 112

This single-seat fighter, which made its debut in 1936, was Heinkel's bid for the Luftwaffe contract which finally went to Messerschmitts and the Bf 109 in the same year. The He 112 was therefore only built in small numbers, approximately 70 being built in all versions. Some were sold to Japan, while others were flown by the Romanians. However, about twelve He 112s were kept as a defence force at Heinkel's Marienehe works and flown by their own test pilots. The aircraft were given false unit markings for propaganda purposes, and this certainly fooled the British, as a number of RAF fighter pilots described combats with He 112s during the Battle of Britain.

The He 112 was considered comparable with, if not better than, the Bf 109. It had a maximum speed of almost 270 mph and a ceiling of almost 28,000 ft. The armament consisted of two MG17 machine-guns and two wing-mounted 20 mm cannon, plus six 22 lb bombs on external racks.

Jagdeinsitzer Heinkel He 112

116

Jagdeinsitzer Heinkel He 112

117

Heinkel – He 113

The He 113 began development in 1937 as an improved version of the He 112 fighter of 1936. It would later be designated He 100, but in March 1939 it reached a record speed of 464 mph. The Luftwaffe were still not interested, mainly due to the aircraft's inability to carry heavy armament and possible handling problems owing to the high landing speeds. The He 113 was used for propaganda purposes, being photographed with false markings and said to be in full production. However this never happened and Heinkel kept twelve He 113s as a protection force at their Rostock-Marienehe factory.

118

The single-seat He 113 had a maximum speed of 416 mph, a ceiling of almost 32,500 ft and a range of 625 miles. Armament consisted of one 20 mm cannon and two MG17 or two MG151 machine-guns.

Heinkel – He 114

First produced in 1936, the He 114 was designed as a reconnaissance floatplane and saw limited service over the Channel and in the North Sea, the Mediterranean and the Adriatic doing coastal reconnaissance work. However, it was outdated by the time the war started, and only about 100 were built for the Luftwaffe.

119

With a crew of pilot and observer/gunner the He 114 had a maximum speed of just over 200 mph and a ceiling of 16,000 ft. Its armament was limited to just one MG15 machine-gun on a movable mounting in the rear cockpit, plus a 2,000 lb bomb load.

Heinkel – He 115

This versatile seaplane first appeared in 1936 and saw service in a number of roles, including reconnaissance, torpedo bombing, minelaying and air-ambulance, however front-line use of the aircraft was mainly limited to Norway, where it attacked Russian convoys in the anti-shipping role. The He 115 proved to be an excellent aircraft, so much so that production continued until 1943, when over 140 were in use with the Luftwaffe.

Crewed by a pilot, observer and radio operator/gunner, the He 115 had a maximum speed of 180 mph and a service ceiling of around 20,000 ft. Armament consisted of two MG15 machine-guns, one in the nose and the other in a dorsal position, a further two MG17 machine-guns in the wings, firing aft, plus a bomb load of over 2,750 lb or one torpedo of 1,100 lb.

120

Courtesy: Lawrence collection.

121

Heinkel He 115

122

123

Heinkel – He 116

Originally produced in 1936 for Luft Hansa as a long-range transoceanic aircraft, the He 116 attracted the interest of the Luftwaffe, who ordered a version for military use. However, the aeroplane's potential was never fully realised, and of fourteen built only eight entered service, being used for photographic and reconnaissance work over the Reich. With a crew of pilot, co-pilot, observer and radio operator the He 116' B' had a maximum speed of just over 200 mph, a ceiling of 21,300 ft and a range of 2,800 miles.
It was unarmed.

Heinkel He 116

124

Henschel – Hs 123

First produced in 1935 by Henschel Flugzeugwerke A.G. as a bomber and ground support aircraft, the Hs 123 was outdated by the outbreak of war but continued in service until late 1944 on the Eastern Front, and as a trainer.

A single-seater, it had a maximum speed of just over 200 mph and a ceiling of 29,500 ft. Its armament consisted of two MG17 machine-guns or two 20 mm cannon, plus a bomb load of almost 1,000 lb.

Henschel Sturzkampfeinsitzer Hs 123

125

Henschel Sturzkampfeinsitzer HS 123

126

Henschel-Sturzkampfeinsitzer HS 123

127

STURZKAMPFFLUGZEUGE VOR DEM START

128

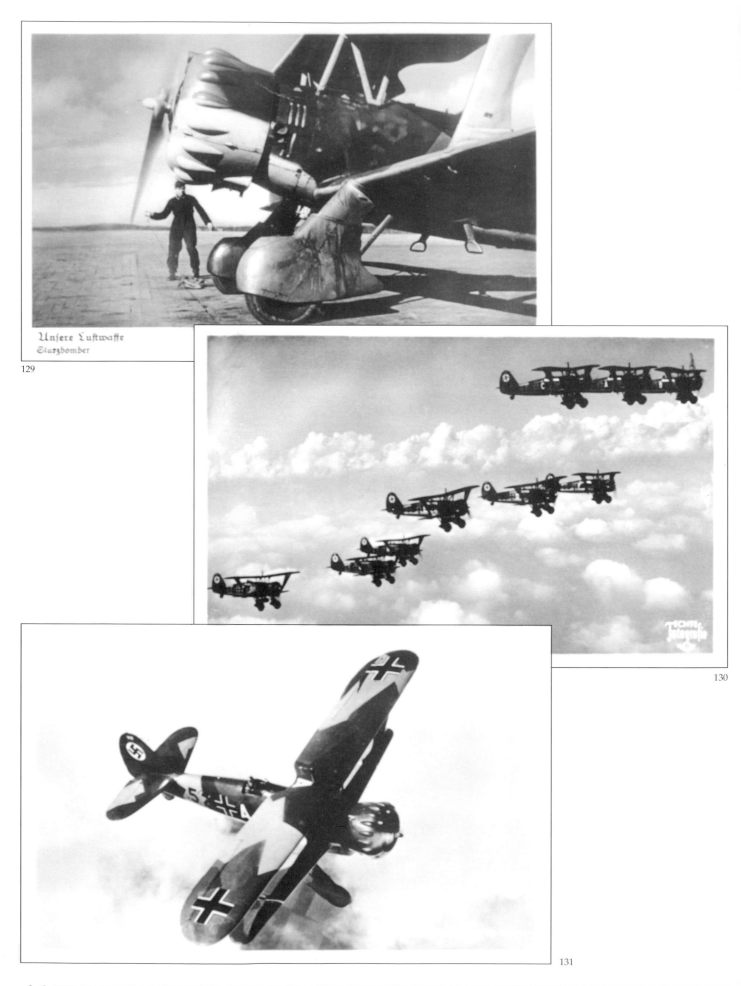

Unsere Luftwaffe
Sturzbomber

129

130

131

132

133

Henschel – Hs 124

The Hs 124 originated in 1937 as a general-purpose aircraft (fighter/light bomber), and early versions/prototypes had a glazed turret in the nose for the front gunner. By 1938 this had been replaced by a completely glazed nose section to accommodate the gunner/bomber, and new engines.

With a crew of pilot, gunner/bomber and rear gunner/radio operator the Hs 124 had a maximum speed of 270 mph, a ceiling of just under 19,700 ft and a range of just over 2,600 miles when fitted with auxiliary fuel tanks. Its armament consisted of either four machine-guns or two machine-guns and two 20 mm cannon; plus a bomb load of up to 6,556 lb.

2 motoriges
Mehrzwecke-
Flugzeug Hs 124

Henschel – Hs 126

A reconnaissance and army support aircraft, the Hs 126 first appeared in 1936 and entered service in 1938. It proved very successful on all fronts until it was replaced in 1940 by the Fw 189. It was subsequently used mainly on the Eastern Front for communications, training and night-attack operations until 1945.

With a crew of pilot and an observer/gunner, the Hs 126 had a maximum speed of almost 200 mph and a ceiling of 27,000 ft. Its armament comprised a single MG17 machine-gun firing forward and a MG15 machine-gun on a movable mounting in the rear cockpit, together with a bomb load of around 330 lb.

Henschel-Mehrzwecke-Flugzeug Hs 126

136

Henschel-Mehrzwecke-Flugzeug Hs 126

137

Henschel-Mehrzwecke-Flugzeug Hs 126

Fl.612

138

Henschel Mehrzweckeflugzeug Hs 126

139

Henschel Mehrzweckeflugzeug Hs126

140

Junkers – Ju(w) 34

First produced by Junkers Flugzeugwerke AG in 1926 as a transport and communications aircraft, the Ju(w) 34 could carry about six passengers or cargo. It saw service during the war as a trainer, a light bomber, an air ambulance and in the communications role. Production ended in 1934, when almost 2,000 had been built.

Crewed by a pilot and observer, the Ju(w) 34 had a maximum speed of almost 170 mph and a ceiling of just under 21,000 ft. It was usually unarmed.

141

142

Junkers – Ju 52

Although it originated in 1930 as a transport and medium bomber, the Ju 52's role as bomber was almost entirely limited to the Spanish Civil War period, when it first entered service with the Condor Legion. Although it had served pre-war as a civil airliner, the sturdy, reliable and very successful Ju 52 became the main transport aircraft of the Luftwaffe for the entire war.

It suffered high losses during the attack on Crete in 1941, the number of experienced transport pilots lost being felt by the Luftwaffe for the rest of the war. Some versions of the Ju 52 were fitted with skis or floats, and it could carry up to 18 passengers. Used post-war by the French Air Force and by the South African and Swiss national airlines, the Ju 52 continued to be built under licence in Spain until the mid 1970s.

With a four-man crew of pilot, observer, radio operator and engineer/gunner it had a maximum speed of almost 170 mph and a service ceiling of 17,500 ft. Armament consisted of two MG15 machine-guns, one in a dorsal position and one in the belly of the aircraft.

143

144

145

146

147

Junkers – Ju 86

First produced in 1934 as a medium bomber, the Ju 86 entered Luftwaffe service in 1936 and was used successfully in Spain and Poland. After 1940 it saw action mainly on the Eastern Front. The R and P versions were very successful as high-altitude reconnaissance aircraft over the Soviet Union, the Mediterranean and the UK.

Crewed by a pilot, observer, radio operator/bomb-aimer and gunner, the Ju 86 had a maximum speed of almost 170 mph and an altitude limit of just under 19,500 ft. Its armament comprised three MG15 machine-guns, one in the nose, one in a dorsal position and one in the belly.

148

149

Junkers-Ju 86

150

Unsere Luftwaffe
Die Flugroute

151

152

153

Falischirme werden angelegt

154

155

156

Courtesy: Lawrence collection

Junkers – Ju 87 "Stuka"

Produced in 1937 as a dive bomber and ground-attack aircraft, the Ju 87 was probably one of the best known and most feared aircraft of the Luftwaffe in the early years of the war. As a dive bomber the psychological effect produced by the siren fitted to its undercarriage was as great as the damage done by its weapons. However, the aircraft was vulnerable to a determined force of defending fighters, and the Stukas suffered heavily during the Battle of Britain, although they were used very successfully in Poland, France, Belgium and Holland.

After 1942 they served mainly on the Eastern Front, where they were successful in the anti-tank role when fitted with 37 mm cannon. Production continued until 1944, when approximately 5,500 had been built in all versions, the Ju 87 continued in the night-attack role until the end of the war. The most highly decorated pilot of the war was Stuka pilot Colonel Hans-Ulrich Rudel.

With a crew of pilot and gunner, the final versions had a maximum speed of over 250 mph, a service ceiling of almost 24,000 ft and a range of over 600 miles. The armament normally consisted of two MG17 machine-guns firing forward and twin MG81 machine-guns in the rear cockpit on a movable mounting, together with a bomb load of almost 4,000 lb.

STURZKAMPFFLIEGER VOR DEM START

157

158

159

Unsere Luftwaffe

160

Sturzkampfflugzeug Ju 87

161

162

Junkers-Ju 87

163

Sturzkampfflugzeug Junkers Ju 87

164

Flugerprobung
einer Ju-87

165

Sturzkamptflugzeug Junkers-Ju 87

166

Sturzkampfflugzeug Junkers-Ju 87

167

Stuka im Angriff

168

Alarm
bei einem
Ju 87-
Geschwader

169

28

P.K.Kriegsberichter Grosse (PBZ)

170

Sturzkampfflugzeug Junkers-Ju 87

171

172

173

Junkers – Ju 88

First produced in 1936, the Ju 88 underwent continuous development from 1936 until 1945. It was a multi-role aircraft, seeing use as medium bomber, dive bomber and torpedo bomber, and in the reconnaissance, ground-support, intruder and mine laying roles. It also proved superior to the Bf 110 as a night fighter.

The Ju 88 entered service with the Luftwaffe in 1939, and production did not end until the factories were overrun in 1945, by which time over 15,000 aircraft had been built in all versions. An extremely successful aircraft, it saw service on all fronts. The early 'A' versions had a crew of four; pilot, observer/bomb-aimer, radio operator/gunner and engineer/gunner, a maximum speed of just under 300 mph and a ceiling of almost 27,000 ft. Armament consisted of seven MG131 machine-guns located at various points, plus a bomb load of almost 8,000 lb.

The later 'G' version night fighter had a crew of pilot, observer, radar operator/gunner and gunner, a maximum speed of just over 400 mph and a ceiling of 32,800 ft. This version was more heavily armed, having six 20 mm cannon (four of which fired forward, and two upwards) together with a MG131 machine-gun in the rear cockpit on a movable mounting.

174

175

Horizontal- und Sturzbomber Junkers-Ju 88

176

Ju 88 werden
zum Einsatz
fertiggemacht

177

178

179

180

181

Horizontal- und Sturzbomber Junkers-Ju 88

182

Horizontal- und Sturzbomber Junkers-Ju 88

183

Junkers – Ju 290

The Junkers Ju 290 was first produced in 1942 as a transport (carrying up to 40 fully equipped troops) or reconnaissance and bomber aircraft. The A-6 version, which could seat up to 50 passengers, was the type intended for use as a personal transport by Hitler and other high-ranking officials. Ju 290 was the military designation given to the Ju 90 civilian aircraft from which it was developed. About 65 Ju 290s were built before 1945.

Crew numbers varied according to the role of the aircraft. In the transport role there were four: pilot, co-pilot, observer and radio operator, while in other roles the crew numbered nine: pilot, co-pilot/navigator, two observers, radio operator, engineer and three gunners.

The Ju 290 had a maximum speed of about 280 mph and a ceiling of approximately 19,700 ft. Armament consisted of seven 20 mm cannon in various positions in the fuselage, and one MG131 machine-gun in the tail, plus a bomb load of approximately 6,600 lb or a number of air-launched missiles.

184

185

Klemm – Kl 25D

Manufactured by the Klemm Leichtflugzeugbau GmbH as a training and liaison aircraft, the Kl 25D first appeared in 1927 and saw some service with the Luftwaffe during the war, some being fitted with skis or floats. Approximately 600 were built before production ended in 1939.

With a pilot and pupil the Kl 25D had a maximum speed of around 100 mph and a ceiling of over 15,500 ft. It was unarmed.

Klemm Schul-, Sport- und Kunstflugzeug Kl 25 D

186

Klemm – WKL 35D

First produced in 1933 as an unarmed liaison and training aircraft, the WKL 35D was used widely at Luftwaffe training schools, normally fitted with a wheeled undercarriage, a version with floats was also produced, but in very small numbers.

With a crew of pilot and pupil it had a maximum speed of about 140 mph and a ceiling of over 14,000 ft.

Klemm WKL 35

187

188

Messerschmitt – Me Bf 108 "Taifun"

First produced by the Bayerische Flugzeugwerke A.G. in 1934 as an unarmed liaison and communications aircraft, the Bf 108 also served as an air ambulance and utility aircraft, and over 1,000 had been built when production ceased in 1944. It was an excellent design, and served on all fronts throughout the war.

The Bf 108 could carry a pilot and up to three passengers: it had a maximum speed of 195 mph, a ceiling of just over 20,300 ft and a range of 620 miles.

Schnellreise- und Umschulungsflugzeug Messerschmitt „Taifun"

189

190

191

Schnellreiseflugzeug Messerschmitt „Taifun"

Messerschmitt – Me Bf 109

The classic Bf 109 single-seat fighter was to become the main fighter aircraft of the Luftwaffe. Having made its first appearance in 1935, it proved very successful and saw action in Spain with the Condor Legion from 1937.

During the war more than 30,000 109s were produced in different versions, seeing service on all fronts, the type being used not only as a fighter but also in the ground support, fighter/bomber and night-attack roles. Like the Spitfire it was not an easy aircraft to fly, its narrow track undercarriage causing many accidents during landing and taxying.

Although the Focke-Wulf Fw 190 was a better aircraft, most of the Luftwaffe fighter aces scored their kills in the Bf 109 and preferred it to the Fw 190, which, in the final analysis, proves that it is the skill of the pilot that counts.

The final versions of the Bf 109 had a maximum speed of almost 350 mph and a service ceiling of just under 38,000 ft. Armament varied, but on the later G version it usually consisted of one 20 mm or 30 mm cannon and two MG131 machine-guns.

Jagdeinsitzer Messerschmitt Me 109

192

Jagdeinsitzer Messerschmitt Me 109 · Vorbereitung zum Feindflug

193

Jagdeinsitzer Messerschmitt Me 109

194

Jagdeinsitzer Messerschmitt Me 109

195

Jagdeinsitzer Messerschmitt Me 109

196

Unsere Luftwaffe

197

198

199

Messerschmitt – Me Bf 110

Produced in 1938 as a heavy fighter for bomber escort duties, the Bf 110 was also used for ground-attack, fighter/bomber, night fighter and occasionally liaison and reconnaissance duties. It performed well in Poland and France early in the war, but the G version was probably the most successful of the series, being used to great effect as a night fighter later in the war. Over 6,000 in all versions had been built by 1945.

With a crew of pilot and observer/gunner or pilot, observer/gunner and radar operator/gunner, the Bf 110 had a maximum speed of around 350 mph and a ceiling of just under 36,000 ft. Armament consisted of two 20 mm or 30 mm cannon firing forward and twin 81Z machine-guns in the rear of the cockpit on a movable mounting.

200

201

202

203

Zerstörer Messerschmitt Me 110

204

205

Messerschmitt – Me Bf 110 "Jaguar"

This was a development of the Bf 110 and was designed as a long-range bomber. It incorporated a glazed nose section to accommodate the bomb-aimer. The armament was altered to three 20 mm cannon and two machine-guns, but other details remained the same as the standard Bf 110.

206

207

Siebel – Fh 104 "Hallore"

First manufactured in 1937 by Siebel Flugzeugwerke K.G. as a communications and liaison aircraft, the Fh 104 also served as a transport for high-ranking personnel being able to carry up to four passengers. Approximately 50 Fh 104s were built for the Luftwaffe.

Crewed only by the pilot, the unarmed Fh 104 had a maximum speed of almost 220 mph and a ceiling of over 21,500 ft.

Schnellreiseflugzeug Fh 104

208

Siebel – Si 202 "Hummel"

Manufactured as a side-by-side light training aircraft, the unarmed Si 202 had a maximum speed of almost 100 mph and a ceiling of just over 14,000 ft.

Klein-Kabinenflugzeug Si 202 Hummel

209

Siebel – Si 204

Originated in 1941 as a communications and training aircraft, the Si 204 saw much service with the Luftwaffe as a trainer, light transport and air ambulance.
In addition some saw limited use in the night-attack role.

With a two-man crew of pilot and observer, the Si 204 could carry up to eight passengers. It had a maximum speed of almost 200 mph and a ceiling of almost 21,000 ft. It did not usually carry armament.

Si 204

210

Personalities & Places

Hauptmann BAUMBACH

211

Lt-Colonel Werner Baumbach

Werner Baumbach was born on 27 December 1916 in Cloppenburg, and at the age of 19 having already acquired his glider pilot's licence, he joined the Luftwaffe and began training at Berlin in April 1936. When war broke out in 1939 Baumbach served as a bomber pilot during the attacks on France, Holland and Belgium. He won the Knight's Cross of the Iron Cross in May 1940 while still a Leutnant, and he was then transferred to Norway, where, promoted to Oberstleutnant, he was extremely successful in attacking Allied convoys. He received the Oakleaves in July 1941 and in 1942 he was decorated with the Swords.

Towards the end of 1942 he was transferred to the Mediterranean, where he found conditions to be less than perfect owing to poor organisation, something which he soon pointed out to his superiors, who were not impressed with his outspokenness. Indeed, Werner Baumbach was lucky to survive the war not as a result of dangerous missions, but as a result of his complaints and disagreement with the High Command over the conduct of the War. Nevertheless, he was the most highly decorated and successful German bomber pilot of the war, with over 300,000 tons of shipping sunk.

He left Germany in 1948 and worked in Argentina as a technical advisor. In October 1953 he crashed into the Rio de la Plata near Buenos Aires during a test flight.

212

Oberst Alfred Druschel

Born in Bindsachsen on 4 February 1917, Druschel joined the Luftwaffe in Berlin in 1936. During the early days of the Second World War he served in Poland and then in France flying a Henschel Hs 123 and in September 1939 he won the Iron Cross Second Class, followed by the First Class award in May 1940.

Following a period attacking shipping in the English Channel and targets on the British mainland, Druschel was posted to the Eastern Front in 1941, where successful operations won him the Knight's Cross of the Iron Cross in August of that year. He was promoted to Hauptmann, receiving the Oakleaves to his Knight's Cross in September 1942, and he added the Swords in February 1943. In March 1943 Druschel was again promoted and given his own unit. More success led to further promotion, and in April 1944 he became Oberstleutnant.

In January 1945 Alfred Druschel was reported missing in action near Aachen while flying a Focke-Wulf Fw 190. He was posthumously promoted to Oberst, having flown some 800 missions during his career.

213

Oberst GALLAND

General Adolf Galland

Born in 1912, General Adolf Galland was a man with great foresight and imagination. He commanded 3/J/88 close-support squadron in Spain, and later served in the campaign against Poland in 1939. He then moved to the Western Front, where he succeeded Werner Mölders as General of Fighter Forces in 1941.

In late 1944 Galland had the idea of concentrating all the remaining fighter forces in one massed attack on Allied bombers as they approached the Reich. However Göring opposed the plan, which might well have shown favourable results, and sent the bulk of these aircraft to the West to assist in the forthcoming Battle of the Bulge.

During the last few days of the war Galland commanded JV44, a squadron of Messerschmitt Me 262 jet fighters. He was a strong believer in the Me 262 being used as a fighter rather than a fighter/bomber, the latter requirement held up development of the aircraft. He ended the war with 104 victories to his credit. He worked in Argentina from 1947 until 1955, when he returned to Germany.

HERMANN GÖRING
Generalfeldmarschall

214

Reichsmarschall Hermann Göring

Reichsmarschall Hermann Göring, a man about whom so much has been written, was born the son of a diplomat in Bavaria in 1893. He served with distinction during the First World War, initially with the infantry and later with the air force, where he proved an excellent commander and pilot.

Following the German surrender in 1918 he lived in Sweden and Denmark, returning to Germany in 1922, when he first met Adolf Hitler in Munich. Subsequently his rise in the Nazi Party was swift, and when Hitler came to power in 1933 Göring was appointed Reichs Commissioner for Aviation.

Hitler and Göring were to remain friends through thick and thin until the spring of 1945, when a telegram he sent to Hitler in which he offered to head negotiations with the Allies for a German surrender, was deliberately twisted and misrepresented by Göring's 'arch enemy' Martin Bormann. He was consequently stripped of all power by Hitler, and so, following his trial, the loyal and devoted Göring committed suicide in his cell on 15 October 1945, before the death sentence could be carried out.

215

General Gordon M. Gollob

General Gordon M. Gollob born in Vienna in 1912. After serving as an instructor with the Austrian Air Force, he later served in the Luftwaffe during the campaigns against Poland, Norway, Britain and on the Eastern Front. A man with great ability, both technically and as a pilot, he was very involved in the development of jet and rocket powered aircraft. He ended his career with 150 victories, nine of which were scored on one day on the Eastern Front.

216

Oberst Hermann Graf

Born in Eugen in 1912, Hermann Graf trained and worked as a government clerk. He was a keen glider pilot before acquiring his powered-aircraft licence in 1936. In 1938, when war seemed inevitable and more trained pilots were needed, he was selected for the Luftwaffe and served in the Mediterranean and on the Eastern Front.

His career as an 'Ace' did not start until 1942, and he received the Knight's Cross of the Iron Cross in January of that year. In May he added the Oakleaves and only two days later he was awarded the Swords, receiving the Diamonds in September 1942, when he had a total of 106 victories to his credit.

An extremely skilful and calculating pilot, liked and admired by his men and other fellow officers, Hermann Graf also served in the defence of Germany. He ended the war with over 200 victories to his credit. He spent five years in Russian prisons following his surrender to the Americans, who handed him over. He died in 1988 after a long illness.

217

Major Hartmann Grasser

Major Hartmann Grasser was born in Graz, Austria, on 23 August 1914. He was already a qualified pilot when Austria became part of the Reich in 1938, and he was inducted into the Luftwaffe before the outbreak of war. Grasser went on to serve in the campaign against France and achieved considerable success flying a Bf 110 during the Battle of Britain, which was no mean feat, as this particular aircraft suffered quite badly during that period.

In February 1941 Grasser was transferred, and served with Oberst Mölders before moving to the Eastern Front, where he was given his own command. By September 1941 he had won the Knight's Cross of the Iron Cross, with 29 victories. Later he was transferred to North Africa, where combat was tougher than on the Eastern Front, but despite this his score reached 103 victories by the end of August 1943, winning him the Oakleaves to his Knight's Cross. Transferred again, this time back to France, he joined the staff of Adolf Galland and distinguished himself in the rebuilding of the Luftwaffe's reserves.

Major Grasser survived the war only to be handed over to the Russians, and spent some four years in extremely severe prison conditions. When released in 1949 he left Germany and worked in India and the Middle East, returning later to pursue an industrial career. Grasser is yet another example of a courageous officer who won the respect of his fellow airmen and achieved the 'Ace' status.

218

Oberst Joachim Helbig

Oberst Joachim Helbig was born in Böhn in September 1915. Following service with the Army he entered the Luftwaffe in 1936, and went on to gain a reputation flying the Junkers Ju 88, which he did for most of the war.

Helbig served in Poland, Norway, the Mediterranean and later during the Normandy landings. He was among the most successful bomber pilots in the Luftwaffe, particularly in the anti-shipping role, where he sank a total of some 180,000 tons of Allied ships. He survived the war, being captured by the Americans at its end.

Oberst Hajo HERRMANN   Photo Bleibtreu, Bonn

219

Colonel Hans Joseph Herrmann

Colonel Hans Joseph Herrmann was born in Kiel in 1913 and entered service with the bomber wing of the Luftwaffe. In 1940 he won the Knight's Cross for his great success in attacking shipping. In 1942 he transferred to night fighters where he again excelled. One of his many good ideas was the development of 'Wild Boar' tactics where night fighters flying at higher altitudes than the attacking bombers could see their targets silhouetted against flak, flares and searchlights from the ground. This method was so successful that it eventually became standard practice for all night fighter units. Herrmann was captured by the Russians in 1945 and spent some ten years in prison.

Major IHLEFELD

220

Oberst Herbert Ihlefeld

Oberst Herbert Ihlefeld, born in Pomerania in June 1914, he entered service with the Luftwaffe early enough to serve with the Condor Legion in Spain, and ended that campaign with seven victories.

During the Second World War he served mainly on the Western Front. Ihlefeld went on to become a highly decorated officer, with over 1,000 missions and 103 victories to his credit. Many young pilots benefited from his vast experience and advice.

221

Generalfeldmarschall KESSELRING

Generalfeldmarschall Albert Kesselring

Generalfeldmarschall Albert Kesselring, born the son of a school teacher in Bavaria in 1885, distinguished himself during the First World War. Following the surrender in 1918 he remained in the Army, and in 1933 transferred to the Luftwaffe, where he played an important role during the early build-up of that organisation.

He commanded 1st Air Fleet during the attacks on Poland and 2nd Air Fleet during the invasion of France and the Battle of Britain, he was in favour of turning the air war to attacks on London, rather than continuing the bombing of RAF airfields and installations which could have destroyed resistance and given the Luftwaffe air superiority.

Kesselring commanded very successful air operations against the Russians in 1941 and the air war against Malta. He favoured a paratroop invasion of the island, which would probably have succeeded and in turn would have saved heavy losses of supplies to Rommel in North Africa. However, the plan was not approved and the stranglehold on shipping continued.

222

Oberst Gunther Lützow

Born in Kiel on 4 September 1912, Gunther Lützow came from a background with strong military connections. He became attracted to a military career, and joined the Luftwaffe in its early days. Lützow served with the Condor Legion in Spain and returned to Germany decorated. Following his success in Spain, he imparted valuable tactical knowledge acquired there to young Luftwaffe trainees in Germany.

He later served during the attacks on Britain, and won the Knight's Cross of the Iron Cross in September 1940, received the Oakleaves in July 1941 and the Swords in October of that year following his 92nd victory. After this a number of staff postings came his way. A man of strong moral values, he more than once faced hostility from his superiors by voicing and defending complaints from the man in the field.

Gunther Lützow joined Adolf Galland and the other few surviving 'Aces' flying Messerschmitt Me 262s in the last days of the war. He was reported missing in action after attacking American bombers near Donauwörth on 24 April 1945, ending his career with 108 victories scored during 300 missions. Lützow was described by his peers as having every best quality expected in a German officer, he was liked and admired by all who knew him.

Hauptmann Hans-Joachim Marseille
Träger des Eichenlaubs mit Schwertern und Brillanten
zum Ritterkreuz des Eisernen Kreuzes

223

Hauptmann Hans-Joachim Marseille

Hauptmann Hans-Joachim Marseille was undoubtedly one of the greatest fighter pilots of all time. Born in Berlin in 1919, he continued the family tradition of a military career when he joined the Luftwaffe in late 1938. Although his early service was marked by a lack of discipline, for which he was reprimanded more than once, the young Marseille was a naturally gifted flyer and really began to show his ability towards the end of the French campaign, winning himself the Iron Cross Second Class in September 1940. Shortly after this he was posted to North Africa, where his numerous exploits became legendary.

In February 1942 he won the Knight's Cross of the Iron Cross having brought his score up to 50 victories, and in June of the same year he received the Oakleaves with a total of 75 victories. Within two weeks he was awarded the coveted Swords, having achieved over 100 victories, and in early September he won the Diamonds to his Knight's Cross.

Finally, on 30 September 1942, while returning to base his Bf 109 suffered engine problems and Marseille left it too late to bale out. When he finally did try to do so he was so weakened by the fumes in the cockpit that he was thrown against the rear of the aircraft and fell to his death with an unopened parachute. Much respected and admired by all his comrades, Marseille was a national hero and assured of his place among the few really great 'Aces' of the Luftwaffe.

Generalfeldmarschall
MILCH

224

Generalfeldmarschall Erhard Milch

Generalfeldmarschall Erhard Milch was born in 1892 the son of a Jewish chemist in the Rhur area. Milch had served with distinction during the First World War and was shattered by the German surrender in 1918. Following impressive work with Junkers Airways he became one of the directors of the newly formed Luft Hansa in 1925.

When he met Hitler in 1930 he was so impressed by the ideas of National Socialism that he began to make regular donations to the Party. When Hitler came to power in 1933, Milch's loyalty paid dividends in his appointment as Secretary of State for Aviation.

A ruthless, clever, and ambitious man, Erhard Milch played no small part in the build-up and development of the Luftwaffe acting as 'deputy' to Göring. Promotion came quickly; he received the Knight's Cross and was promoted to Feldmarschall in 1940, following the French defeat. However, Milch finally lost favour with Hitler over the Me 262 jet fighter programme in 1944, after which time he occupied only token positions.

225

General Werner Mölders

General Werner Mölders, born the son of a school teacher in 1913, was to become a hero of the Luftwaffe and the German people. While serving with the Condor Legion in Spain he developed fighter tactics that would change the face of air warfare forever.

Having transferred from the infantry to the Luftwaffe in 1934, he proved to be a brilliant pilot and quickly won promotion, receiving the Knight's Cross with Oakleaves and Swords in 1941. Mölders was a charming man who was admired and respected by junior airmen and senior officers at all levels.

His death was a great loss to the Luftwaffe; when his aircraft crashed near Breslau in November 1941, as he was making his way to the funeral of General Ernst Udet. Mölders had over 100 victories to his credit when he died aged 28.

226

Oberst Walter Oesau

Oberst Walter Oesau, born in Holstein in June 1913, served with the Condor Legion and returned to Germany with eight victories to his credit. He served in operations on the Western Front in the early part of the Second World War but by mid 1941 he had been moved to the Eastern Front. Following a very successful period, when his score reached 80 victories, he was posted back to the West towards the end of 1941.

Shortly after this Oesau was removed from combat flying, being considered too valuable in other areas to risk his being killed. However, in 1943 with the tide beginning to turn, he was returned to active service. He was killed in combat on 11 May 1944, when his score stood at 123 victories.

227

Colonel Hans Philipp

Colonel Hans Philipp, an experienced fighter pilot which the Luftwaffe could ill afford to lose, was killed in action on 8 October 1943 with 206 victories to his credit. The loss of such pilots, who could not be replaced as the training schools had been drained of both their best instructors and pupils for earlier campaigns, was to become one of the greatest factors in the defeat of the Luftwaffe.

228

Generalfeldmarschall Wolfram Freiherr von Richthoffen

Generafieldmarschall Wolfram Freiherr von Richthoffen was born in 1895. He entered service during the last days of the First World War under the command of his cousin 'The Red Baron', and later under Hermann Göring. Wolfram ended the conflict with eight victories to his credit. Transferring from the Army to the Luftwaffe in 1933, he went on to join Hugo Sperrle in command of the Condor Legion in Spain. During his time there he came up with many good ideas, including close air support for ground troops, something which would be put to good use in the approaching war.

When war broke out in 1939 he played an important part in the attacks on Poland, Holland, Belgium and France. Later he helped save the day during the costly invasion of Crete and again distinguished himself in Russia. Richthoffen made considerable contributions to the German advance in Russia with his 8th Air Corps, and when given the responsibility of supplying Stalingrad from the air he did all that was possible. As a result was promoted to Feldmarschall. When moved to Italy he almost succeeded, with limited resources, in turning back the Allied invasion in 1943. However his health was now failing owing to a brain tumour, and after 1944 he could not return to active duty. A man highly regarded by his fellow officers, and one of the Luftwaffe's greatest commanders he died quietly in Austria in July 1945.

229

Generalfeldmarschall SPERRLE

Generalfeldmarschall Hugo Sperrle

Generalfeldmarschall Hugo Sperrle, born in 1885, served through the 1914-18 war and ended that period as the senior officer for flying units with the Seventh Army. Later, when the Spanish Civil War broke out in 1936, Sperrle commanded the Condor Legion which Hitler sent to assist Franco, here he developed tactics which would be used during the Second World War.

Sperrle held joint command of the Luftwaffe during the invasion of Norway and during the early days of the Battle of Britain. Had his ideas on the conduct of the air war with Britain been adopted, it is almost certain that the RAF would have been defeated. After 1940 he began to lose interest in the conflict and concentrated on enjoying a life of luxury in France, making no real contribution to the war effort after this time. Following his capture in 1945 and release in 1948 he lived in Munich until his death in 1953.

Major Walter STORP   Photo J. P. Böhm, München

230

Generalmajor Walter Storp

Generalmajor Walter Storp was born in East Prussia in February 1910. He began his pilot training in 1933 at Warnemünde, and took part in the attacks on Poland, flying a Bf 110 and winning the Iron Cross Second Class.

After the fall of Poland he switched over to bombers and served during the invasions of Norway, France (including Dunkirk), in the attacks against England, on the Eastern Front and later in the Mediterranean. In late 1944 he was promoted to General der Kampfflieger. After being taken prisoner at the end of the war he was released in 1948. This highly competent officer, always well respected by his peers, died in August 1981, aged 71.

231

Generaloberst Ernst UDET

General Ernst Udet

General Ernst Udet, born in 1896, was the highest-scoring German pilot to survive the First World War, with 60 victories to his credit. A friend of Hermann Göring from that time, he was a man who loved to fly, and was perhaps not the best choice for the offices he would later hold.

He joined the Luftwaffe in 1935, being appointed Chief of the Technical Office in 1936 and Director General of Equipment in 1939. In all he had some 226 departments under his control, something far beyond his management capabilities.

Udet was a charming man well liked and respected by his superiors, but he unfortunately chose the wrong aircraft for production and development to replace existing aircraft, which cost Germany valuable time. Furthermore he exaggerated performance levels and numbers of aircraft, with the result that Germany went to war three or four years sooner than Hitler would have done had he known the true strength of the Luftwaffe.

Generaloberst Udet, Oberst Galland und Oberst Mölders

232

Udet, Galland and Mölders

This postcard which is autographed by General Adolf Galland, shows General Ernst Udet (left), General Galland (centre) and General Werner Mölders (right), and can be dated prior to November 1941, which was when General Udet committed suicide as a result of problems and pressure of work from his many departments.

General Mölders was killed in a flying accident while on his way to General Udet's funeral, where he was to be a member of the guard of honour. Only General Galland survived the war.

233

Major Helmut Wick

Major Helmut Wick was born in Mannheim in 1915 the son of an agricultural engineer. He scored his first victories on the Western Front while serving under Werner Mölders, and won the Knight's Cross in 1940, going on to have his own command later that year. Disliking discipline, and always something of a rebel, even in his youth, Helmut Wick was popular with most junior officers for these very reasons.

He was killed in action near the Isle of Wight on 28 November 1940. With 56 victories to his credit, he was the second-highest-scoring German fighter pilot at that point in the war.

Berlin, Reichsluftfahrt-Ministerium   Wessely-Foto

234

Luftwaffe headquarters in the Wilhelmstrasse, Berlin. Apart from the removal of the national symbols from the pillars, the building remains virtually unchanged today.

A fine view of an accommodation block and well-kept grounds at one of the many Luftwaffe bases.

Gruß aus einem Fliegerhorst

235

Everyday Life

236

The daily queue for food and tables in the mess — nothing changes.

237

The reverse of this card is titled 'Ein Sonntagsbraten' (A Sunday Roast). It shows conditions in the field.

238

The caption on the reverse of this card reads: 'Men from gound personnel checking the engines'.

239

Caption on reverse reads: 'Sleeping on the bombs during breaks is particularly good'.

Appendix

The following information has been taken from the reverse of all postcards shown on these pages (together with dates of postmarks where they exist), and should be accepted as acknowledgement and credit to all photographers, publishers and aircraft companies.

This information may be referenced by use of the numbers located next to each postcard.

Finally thanks to my friends Peter Lawrence, who has kindly allowed the use of several postcards from his own collection, and to Jeff Gilbert for his help and patience.

1 Kunstverlag: Heinrich Trittler, Frankfurt a. Main, Goethestr. 37. Photo: Kaiser
2 Verlag: Hilde Seifert-Eckert, St Andreasberg. Echte Photographie.
3 Verlag: Klinke & Co., Berlin W 8, Leipziger Str. 24. Echtes Foto.
4 Driesen-Verlag. Berlin N 58, Echte Fotografie.
   Posted: 8.9.39.
5 Photo: Hoffmann, München, Friedrichstr. 34. Echte Fotografie.
6 Verlag: Klinke & Co., Berlin W 8, Leipziger Str. 24.
   Posted: 31.8.36.
7 Heinz Schröter, Fotographie.
8 Heinz Schröter, Fotographie.
9 Heinz Schröter, Fotographie.
   Posted: 8.8.38.
10 Heinz Schröter, Fotographie.
   Posted: 4.5.40.
11 Fotovervielfältigung: H. C. Stöckel, Hannover 1, Postfach 53.
12 Driesen-Verlag. Berlin N 58.
13 Fotovervielfältigung: H. C. Stöckel, Hannover 1, Postfach 53.
14 Arado-Bildstelle. d. RLM Echte Photographie.
   Posted: 31.8.40.
15 RLM Berlin. Echte Photo.
   Posted: 14.9.39.
16 Arado-Bildstelle. d. RLM Echte Photographie.

15

17 Arado-Bildstelle. d. RLM Verlag: Bruno Hausmann, Kassel.
Posted: 28.12.42.

18 Fotostöckel, Hannover 1. Echtes Foto.

19 Driesen-Verlag. Berlin C2. Echte Fotografie.

20 Film·Foto·Verlag, Berlin SW68. Echt Photo.

21 PK-Aufnahme: Aubele (Sch). Echte Photographie.

22 Verlag: Thorsden Jun. Hamburg 1. Deutsches Postkartenbildwerk.

23 Kunstverlag: Carl Friedrich Fangmeier, Magdeburg. Echte Photographie.

24 Kunstverlag: Carl Friedrich Fangmeier, Magdeburg. Echte Photographie.

25 Bücker-Flugzeugbau GmbH., Rangsdorf Bei Berlin. Echte Photographie.

26 Bücker-Flugzeugbau GmbH., Rangsdorf Bei Berlin. Gustav Petermann.

27 Wehrmacht-Fotokarten-Spezialverlag HORN, Gotha. Foto: B. Mitschke.
Posted: 24.11.37.

28 Franckh-Verlag Stuttgart-O. Echte Photographie.
Posted: 2.5.37.

29 Driesen-Verlag. Berlin N 58. Ruge-Foto. SAD-Postkarte.

30 Fotokarten-Spezialverlag HORN, Gotha.
Posted: 25.3.39.

31 Franckh-Verlag Stuttgart-O. Kosmos.

32 Driesen-Verlag. Berlin N 58. Ruge-Foto.

33 Fleiger-Fotokarten-Spezialverlag HORN, Gotha. Luftbild: Hans Schaller.
Posted: 7.4.42.

34 Fleiger-Fotokarten-Spezialverlag HORN, Gotha. Luftbild: Hans Schaller.
Posted: 1.5.44.

35 Werkefoto Dornier. Echte Photographie.

36 Driesen-Verlag. Berlin C2. Echte Fotografie.

37 *Der Adler*: die grosse Luftwaffen-Illustrierte.

38 Fotovervielfältigung: H. C. Stöckel, Hannover 1, Postfach 53. Echte Foto.
Posted: 27.10.42.

39 Fleiger-Fotokarten-Spezialverlag HORN, Gotha. Luftbild: Hans Schaller.
Posted: 20.6.40.

40 Verlag: Julius Simonsen, Oldenberg in Holstein. Echte Photographie.

41 Franckh-Verlag Stuttgart-O. Kosmos.
Posted: 2.5.38.

42 *Der Adler*: die grosse Luftwaffen-Illustrierte.

FOTO-Serie - Unsere Luftwaffe
Zweimotoriges Kampfflugzeug Dornier Do 17
im Manöver

Nr. 227 Flieger-Fotokarten-Spezialverlag HORN, Gotha, gegr 1893 · Nachdruck verboten
Luftbild: Hans Schaller, freigeg. d. R. L. M. Nr. 2516

HORN's echte Foto - Qualitätskarte - eine Erinnerung für's Leben

39

43 Film·Foto·Verlag, Berlin SW68.
    Posted: 13.11.41.
44 Photo: Hoffmann, München, Friedrichstr. 34.
45 Film·Foto·Verlag, Berlin SW68.
46 Fleiger-Fotokarten-Spezialverlag HORN, Gotha.
47 Fleiger-Fotokarten-Spezialverlag HORN, Gotha.
    Posted: 4.5.42.
48 Driesen-Verlag. Berlin C2. Echte Fotografie.
49 Kunstverlagsanstalt: Bruno Hansmann, Kassel. Echte Photographie.
50 Kunstverlag: Carl Friedrich Fangmeier, Magdeburg. Echte Photographie.
51 Photo: Hoffmann, München, Friedrichstr. 34. Echte Fotographie.
52 Foto: Gerhard Fieseler Werke. Echte Photographie.
    Posted: 18.1.44.
53 Verlag: Klinke & Co., Berlin W 8, Leipziger Str. 24.
    Posted: 30.9.35.
54 Franckh-Verlag Stuttgart-O. Kosmos.
    Posted: 12.1.38.
55 Spezialverlag Albert Horn, Gotha. Echte Fotografie.
    Posted: 28.10.37.
56 Ross-Verlag, Berlin SW68. Echt Photo.
    Posted: 28.5.41.
57 Kunstverlag: Carl Friedrich Fangmeier, Magdeburg. Echte Photographie.
58 Photo: Hoffmann, München, Friedrichstr. 34. Echte Fotografie.
59 Kunstverlag: Carl Friedrich Fangmeier, Magdeburg. Echte Photographie.
    Posted: 20.3.37.
60 Posted: 16.6.37.
61 Kunstverlagsanstalt: Bruno Hansmann, Kassel. Echte Photographie.
62 Kunstverlagsanstalt: Bruno Hansmann, Kassel. Echte Photographie.
63 Franckh-Verlag Stuttgart-O.d.RLM Kosmos.
64 Fotovervielfältigung: H. C. Stöckel, Hannover 1, Postfach 53. Echte Photographie.
65 Kunstverlagsanstalt: Bruno Hansmann, Kassel. Echte Photographie.
    Posted: 8.12.39.
66 Kunstverlag: Carl Friedrich Fangmeier, Magdeburg. Echte Photographie.
67 Driesen-Verlag. Berlin N 58. S.A.D. Postkarte.
68 Posted: 30.6.40.

69 Echt Photo. Posted: 14.11.40.
70 Verlag Thür: Press-Photo, B. Mitschke, Oberhof (Thür.) durch RLM
   Echte Photographie.
   Posted: 8.3.41.
71 Verlag d. O.L.F. Echte Photographie. D.T.V.
72 Driesen-Verlag. Berlin C2. d. OLF Echte Fotografie.
73 Trinks & Co., Leipzig. Echte Photographie. Teco.
74 Echte Photographie. Posted: 22.10.43.
75 Driesen-Verlag. Berlin C2. Echte Fotografie.
76 Echte Photographie. Posted: 20.10.44.
77 Verlag d. O.L.F. S.B.
78 Trinks & Co., Leipzig. Echte Photographie. Teco.
79 Echtes Foto. d. OLF
80 Echte Photographie. d. OLF
81 Kosmos. Posted: 14.1.38.
82 Echte Photographie. Posted: 28.4.37.
83 Verlag: *Die Wehrmacht*, GmbH, Berlin W8. Kronenstrasse 37.
   Phot: Schaller, Berlin.
   Posted: 3.12.38.
84 Echt Foto. Posted: 20.9.37.
85 Echte Photographie. Photo: Alex Stöcker.
86 Driesen-Verlag. Berlin N 58. Foto: Heinz Schröter, Osnabrück. Echte Photographie.
87 Hermann Trautwein, Nürnberg-O. Echte Fotokarte.
   Posted: 6.9.39.
88 Driesen-Verlag. Berlin N 58. Echte Fotografie.
   Posted: 15.2.37.
89 Unmarked
90 Verlag: Julius Simonsen, Oldenberg in Holstein. Echte Photographie.
91 Film·Foto·Verlag, Berlin SW68. Echte Photo.
92 Reichsluftfahrtministerium, Berlin.
   Posted: 8.2.39.
93 Kunstfoto: A Klein, Kiel, Holstenstr. 104. Echte Photographie.
   Posted: 12.9.40.
94 Film·Foto·Verlag, Berlin SW68. Echte Photo.
95 Kunstfoto: A Klein, Kiel, Holstenstr. 104. Echte Photographie.
   Posted: 18.11.36.

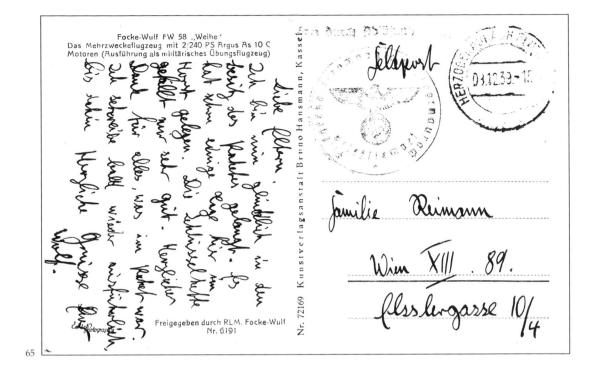

96 Verlag: Julius Simonsen, Oldenberg i. Holstein. Echte Photographie.
97 Ernst Heinkel Flugzeugwerke GmbH, Rostock. Echte Photographie.
98 Franckh-Verlag Stuttgart-O. d. RLM. Kosmos.
99 Driesen-Verlag. Berlin C2. Echte Fotografie.
100 Echt Foto. Posted: 14.9.41.
101 Fleiger-Fotokarten-Spezialverlag HORN, Gotha. Foto: Hans Schaller.
      Posted: 19.7.42.
102 Fleiger-Fotokarten-Spezialverlag HORN, Gotha. Luftbild: Hans Schaller.
      Posted: 25.11.39.
103 Driesen-Verlag. Berlin N 58. Echte Fotografie.
      Posted: 12.1.40.
104 Echte Photographie.
105 Foto-Stöckel, Hannover 1, Postfach 53. d.RLM
      Posted: 20.1.42.
106 Fotovervielfältigung: H. C. Stöckel, Hannover 1, Postfach 53. Echte Foto.
      Posted: 4.11.42.
107 Trinks & Co., Leipzig. d. RLM Echte Photographie. Teco.
      Posted: 24.7.40.
108 *Der Adler*: die grosse Luftwaffen-Illustrierte.
109 Foto-Stöckel, Hannover 1, Postfach 53. Echtes Foto.
110 Bernhard Mitschke, Aktueller Bildverlag, Oberhof Thür. d.RLM Echte Fotografie.
111 Foto-Stöckel, Hannover. Echtes Stöckelfoto.
112 *Der Adler*: die grosse Luftwaffen-Illustrierte.
113 Verlag: Kurt Hecht, Wernigerode. d. OLF.
114 Verlag: Kurt Hecht, Wernigerode. d. OLF.
115 Verlag: Kurt Hecht, Wernigerode. d. OLF.
116 Posted: 14.10.38.
117 Kunstverlag: Carl Friedrich Fangmeier, Magdeburg. Echte Photographie.
      Posted: 30.5.38.
118 Verlag Thür: Press-Photo, B. Mitschke, Oberhof (Thür.) durch RLM Echt Photo.
119 Photo: Hoffmann, München, Friedrichstr. 34. Echte Fotografie.
120 Driesen-Verlag. Berlin C2. Echte Fotografie.
121 Trinks & Co., Leipzig. d. RLM. Echte Photographie. Teco.
      Posted: 16.2.41.
122 Film·Foto·Verlag, Berlin SW68. Echte Photo.

123 Unmarked.
124 Ernst Heinkel Flugzeugwerke G.m.b.H., Seestadt Rostock. Echte Photographie.
125 Driesen-Verlag. Berlin N 58. S.A.D. Postkarte.
126 Echtes Stöckel-foto.
127 Fotovervielfältigung: H. C. Stöckel, Hannover 1, Postfach 53. Echte Fotokarte.
128 Verlag: *Die Wehrmacht*, GmbH, Berlin W 8. Kronenstrasse 37.
   Phot: Gunther Pilz, Berlin.
   Posted: 17.10.39.
129 Ross-Verlag, Berlin SW68. Echt Photo.
   Posted: 22.6.41.
130 Fleiger-Fotokarten-Spezialverlag HORN, Gotha. Luftbild: Hans Schaller. d. RLM.
   Posted: 7.11.40.
131 Photo: Hoffmann, München, Friedrichstr. 34. Echte Fotografie.
132 *Der Adler*: die grosse Luftwaffen-Illustrierte.
133 Fleiger-Fotokarten-Spezialverlag HORN, Gotha. Foto: Hans Schaller.
134 Verlag: Klinke & Co., Berlin W 8, Leipziger Str. 24.
   Posted: 17.10.38.
135 Echte Foto. d. RLM.
136 Photo: Hoffmann, München, Friedrichstr. 34. Echte Fotografie.
137 Henschel Flugzeugwerke A.G., Schönefeld, Kr. Teltow. Luftbild Schaller.
138 Industrie-Fotografen: Klinke & Co., Berlin W 8, Leipziger Str. 24. Echtes Foto.
139 Kunstverlag: Carl Friedrich Fangmeier, Magdeburg. Luftbild Hans Schaller.
140 Driesen-Verlag. Berlin C2. Echte Fotografie.
141 Verlag: Schöning & Co., Lübeck.
   Posted: 20.7.38.
142 Driesen-Verlag. Berlin C2. Foto: Junkers-FM. Echte Fotografie.
143 Kunstverlag: E.A.Schwerdtfeger & Co., AG., Berlin. Foto: Junkers.
144 Spezialverlag Albert Horn, Gotha.
145 Verlag: Julius Simonsen, Oldenberg i. Holstein. Echte Photographie.
146 Foto Junkers-FM. Jllersperger.
147 Foto Junkers-FM. Echte Photographie.
   Posted: 20.4.44.
148 Fotokarten-Spezialverlag HORN, Gotha. Luftbild: Hans Schaller.
   Posted: 12.4.38.
149 Fleiger-Fotokarten-Spezialverlag HORN, Gotha. Foto: Hans Schaller.

150 Kunstverlag: Carl Friedrich Fangmeier, Magdeburg. Echte Photographie.
Posted: 25.9.39.
151 Ross-Verlag, Berlin SW68. Echt Photo.
Posted: 3.12.40.
152 Fleiger-Fotokarten-Spezialverlag HORN, Gotha.
Posted: 14.3.44.
153 Fleiger-Fotokarten-Spezialverlag HORN, Gotha. Luftbild: H. Schaller.
Posted: 16.2.44.
154 Heinz Schröter. 'Deutsche Wehrmacht'.
Posted: 25.11.41.
155 Fleiger-Fotokarten-Spezialverlag HORN, Gotha. H. Schaller. d. RLM.
156 Fleiger-Fotokarten-Spezialverlag HORN, Gotha. Hans Schaller. d. RLM.
157 Verlag: *Die Wehrmacht*, GmbH, Berlin W8. Kronenstrasse 37.
Phot: *Die Wehrmacht* – Pilz, Berlin.
158 Trinks & Co., Leipzig. Echte Photographie. Teco.
159 Bernhard Mitschke, Aktueller Bildverlag, Oberhof (Thür.) Echt Foto.
160 'Ross' Verlag, Berlin SW68. Echt Photo.
Posted: 3.4.41.
161 Fotovervielfältigung: H. C. Stöckel, Hannover 1, Postfach 53. Echtes Foto.
Posted: 30.6.40.
162 RLM. JFM., Dessau. Amag. Echte Photographie.
163 Kunstverlag: Carl Friedrich Fangmeier, Magdeburg. Echte Photographie.
164 RLM. JFM., Dessau. Kosmos.
165 Aufnahme: JFM. Rikki. Echt Fotogravüre.
166 Echte Foto.
167 Ross-Verlag, Berlin SW68. Foto Junkers.
Posted: 28.6.42.
168 Franckh-Verlag Stuttgart-O. d. RLM. Kosmos.
Posted: 26.9.40.
169 JFM. – Tobis. Rikki. Bildpostkarte.
Posted: 8.2.41.
170 Steiniger-Bilddrucke Verlagsgesellschaft m.b.H., Berlin SW 68. Echte Fotografie.
Posted: 14.7.43.
171 Kunstverlagsanstalt: Bruno Hansmann, Kassel. d. RLM. JFM/Dessau.
172 Verlag: Franz Zabel, Dessau – Druck Carl Warnecke, Halle/S.

173 Foto: Schaller.
174 Foto: JFM/PK
175 Film·Foto·Verlag, Berlin SW68. Foto Junkers FM.
176 Driesen-Verlag. Berlin C2. Echte Fotografie.
Posted: 10.10.44.
177 JFM. Rikki. Bildpostkarte.
178 Foto: Junkers-FM, Jllersperger.
179 Foto: Junkers-FM, Jllersperger.
180 Foto: Junkers-FM, Jllersperger.
181 Foto: Junkers-FM, Jllersperger.
182 Photo: Hoffmann, München, Friedrichstr. 34. Echte Fotografie.
183 Film·Foto·Verlag, Berlin SW68. Foto Junkers FM.
184 Foto: Junkers-FM. Echte Photographie.
185 Werkfoto JFA Sparo. Echte fotografie.
186 Verlag: Klinke & Co., Berlin W 8, Leipziger Str. 24.
Posted: 30.1.36.
187 Kunstverlagsanstalt: Bruno Hansmann, Kassel.
188 Amag. Echte Photographie.
189 Ross-Verlag, Berlin SW68. d. RLM. Echt Photo.
Posted: 1.7.41.
190 Messerschmitt A.G. d. RLM.
Posted: 26.9.40.
191 Messerschmitt A.G. Augsburg. d. RLM.
Posted: 3.1.40.
192 Film·Foto·Verlag, Berlin SW68. d. RLM. Echt Photo.
193 'Stöckel' - Wehrmachtarte.
194 Film·Foto·Verlag, Berlin SW68. d. RLM. Echt Photo.
195 Fotovervielfältigung: H. C. Stöckel, Hannover 1, Postfach 53. Echtes Foto.
196 Ross-Verlag, Berlin SW68. d. RLM.
Posted: 30.5.41.
197 Ross-Verlag, Berlin SW68. d. RLM.
Posted: 2.10.42.
198 Fleiger-Fotokarten-Spezialverlag HORN, Gotha. Luftbild: Hans Schaller.
Posted: 5.10.39.
199 Fotovervielfältigung: H. C. Stöckel, Hannover 1, Postfach 53. Echte Fotokarte.

107

200 Fotovervielfältigung: H. C. Stöckel, Hannover 1, Postfach 53. Echtes Foto.
201 Messerschmitt A.G. Foto: Thiel.
    Posted: 21.8.44.
202 Verlag Röhr, Magdeburg (Foto W. Ruge).
    Posted: 15.8.43.
203 Verlag Röhr, Magdeburg (Foto W. Ruge). Echte Photographie.
204 Fotovervielfältigung: H. C. Stöckel, Hannover 1, Postfach 53. Echte Fotokarte.
205 Verlag Röhr, Magdeburg (Foto W. Ruge). Echte Photographie.
206 Bernhard Mitschke, Aktueller Bildverlag, Oberhof (Thür.) d. RLM Echt Photo.
    Posted: 9.8.34.
207 Bernhard Mitschke, Aktueller Bildverlag, Oberhof (Thür.) d. RLM Echt Photo.
208 Echt Photo.
209 Siebel Flugzeugwerke Halle K.G., Halle/S.
210 Kunstverlagsanstalt: Bruno Hansmann, Kassel. Werkfoto Siebel.
211 Photo: Hoffmann, München, Friedrichstr. 34. Echte Fotografie.
212 Verlag Röhr, Magdeburg – PK-Aufn. Hempe. Echte Photographie.
213 Photo: Hoffmann, München, Friedrichstr. 34. Echte Fotografie.
214 Photo: Hoffmann, München, Theresienstr. 74. Echte Fotografie.
215 Photo: Hoffmann, München, Friedrichstr. 34. Echte Fotografie.
216 Photo: Hoffmann, München, Friedrichstr. 34. Echte Fotografie.
217 Photo: Hoffmann, München, Friedrichstr. 34. Echte Fotografie.
218 Photo: Hoffmann, München, Friedrichstr. 34. Echte Fotografie.
219 Photo: Hoffmann, München, Friedrichstr. 34. Echte Fotografie.
220 Photo: Hoffmann, München, Friedrichstr. 34. Echte Fotografie.
221 Photo: Hoffmann, München, Friedrichstr. 34. Echte Fotografie.
222 Verlag Röhr, Magdeburg. Echte Photographie.
223 Film·Foto·Verlag, Berlin SW68. Echt Photo.
224 Photo: Hoffmann, München, Friedrichstr. 34. Echte Fotografie.
225 Photo: Hoffmann, München, Friedrichstr. 34. Echte Fotografie.
226 Photo: Hoffmann, München, Friedrichstr. 34. Echte Fotografie.
227 Photo: Hoffmann, München, Friedrichstr. 34. Echte Fotografie.
228 Photo: Hoffmann, München, Friedrichstr. 34. Echte Fotografie.
229 Photo: Hoffmann, München, Friedrichstr. 34. Echte Fotografie.
230 Photo: Hoffmann, München, Friedrichstr. 34. Echte Fotografie.
231 Photo: Hoffmann, München, Friedrichstr. 34. Echte Fotografie.

232 Film·Foto·Verlag, Berlin SW68. Echt Photo.
233 Photo: Hoffmann, München, Friedrichstr. 34. Echte Fotografie.
234 Postkartenverlag: Felix Setecki, Berlin C2. 'Wessely-' Karten.
235 Kunst-u. Verlagsanstalt A. Weber & Co., Stuttgart. Echte Photographie.
236 *Wehrmacht*: – Günther Pilz. Kosmos.
237 PK-Aufnahme: Eiling (PBZ). Echte Photographie.
238 *Der Adler*: die grosse Luftwaffen-Illustrierte. Aufnahme PK Ketelhohn-Scherl.
239 *Der Adler*: die grosse Luftwaffen-Illustrierte. Aufnahme JFM.
    Posted: 24.8.42.

Bibliography

Jane's All The World's Aircraft **(1933-1945 inclusive)**
C. G. Grey & Leonard Bridgman
(London: Sampson Low, Marston & Company, Ltd.)

Eagles of the Third Reich
Samuel W. Mitcham
(UK: Airlife Publishing Ltd. 1989.)

The Encyclopedia of German Military Aircraft
Brian Philpot
(New York: Park South Books. 1986.)

Pictoral History of the Luftwaffe
Alfred Price FRHistS
(UK: Airlife Publishing Ltd. 1991.)

Aces of the Reich
Gordon Williamson
(London: Arms & Armour Press. 1981.)